SERMON OUTLINES
ON
FAITH,
HOPE,
AND
LOVE

Books by Al Bryant

Climbing the Heights
Day by Day with C. H. Spurgeon
More Sermon Outlines for Special Occasions
More Sermon Outlines on Prayer
New Every Morning
Revival Sermon Outlines
Sermon Outlines for Evangelistic Occasions
Sermon Outlines for Funerals and Other Special Occasions
Sermon Outlines for Lay Leaders
Sermon Outlines on Bible Characters (Old Testament)
Sermon Outlines on Bible Characters (New Testament)
Sermon Outlines on the Attributes of God
Sermon Outlines on the Deeper Life
Sermon Outlines on the Cross of Christ
Sermon Outlines on Faith, Hope, and Love
Sermon Outlines on Family and Home
Sermon Outlines on the Life of Christ
Sermon Outlines on Prayer
Sermon Outlines on Prophetic Themes
Sermon Outlines for Special Occasions
Sermon Outlines for Worship Services
Sourcebook of Poetry

SERMON OUTLINES
ON
FAITH, HOPE, AND LOVE

compiled by
Al Bryant

kregel
PUBLICATIONS

Grand Rapids, MI 49501

Sermon Outlines on Faith, Hope, and Love by Al Bryant

Copyright © 1996 by Kregel Publications, a division of Kregel, Inc., P.O. Box 2607, Grand Rapids, MI 49501. Kregel Publications provides trusted, biblical publications for Christian growth and service. Your comments and suggestions are valued.

Cover and book design: Alan G. Hartman

Library of Congress Cataloging-in-Publication Data
Bryant, Al (1926–
    Sermon outlines on faith, hope, and love / [compiled by] Al Bryant
        p.   cm.
Includes index.
    1. Faith—Biblical teaching—Sermons—Outlines, syllabi, etc. 2. Hope—Biblical teaching—Sermons—Outlines, syllabi, etc. 3. Love—Biblical teaching—Sermons—Outlines, syllabi, etc. I. Bryant, Al, 1926–
BT771.2S44   1996   251'.02—dc20   96-10317
                                                                CIP
ISBN 0-8254-2154-3

        1 2 3 4 5 printing/year 00 99 98 97 96

Printed in the United States of America

CONTENTS

Preface 7

Scripture Index 8

Faith

Faith, Hope, and Love 9

Three Supreme Resolutions for the New Year 10

The Object of Our Faith and Hope 11

Characteristics of Faith 12

Faith in Exercise 13

True Faith and Its Fruits 13

What We Gain by Faith 14

What We Do by Faith 14

Faith 15

Assurance of Faith 15

Facts about Faith 16

The Believer's Growth in Faith 16

A Definition of Faith 17

Fear and Faith 18

Faith's Language 19

Responsiveness of the Lord to Faith 20

Certainties of the Faith 21

The Faith That Transforms the Life 22

Attempting High and Hard Things (Faith in Motion) 23

Increase of Faith 25

Great Faith 25

Having Goals (Faith in Action) 26

The Higher Wisdom (Faith) 27

Faith's Walk 27

On Faith and Faithfulness 29

Faith—Life's Greatest Venture 30

Faith Not Fear 31

The End of Faith 32

Your Faith 33

Victorious Faith 33

Hope

The Christian's Hope 36

Cheer Up! 36

The Hope of the Gospel 37

The Saint's Hope 38
The Reality of Hope 39
Cheerfulness 40
Christian Hope Accounted For 41
Hope 44
Hopelessness 45
Depression 46

Love
Bands of Love 47
Love of the Whole Man 48
How to Create Christian Love 49
Love Shown in the Mutual Care of Christians 50
Living in Love 51
Keep Out of Debt 51
A Love Gift 52
The New Commandment 53
The Badge of Discipleship 54
Love Is of God 54
The Love of the Infinite God 55
Love: Our Relative Duty to Believers 55
God Is Love 56
Love's Attitude 56
Love's Ministry 58
Love's Ministry 58
Love's Traits 60
Love's Recognition 62
Love's Mantle 63

As the opening outlines in this compilation reveal so eloquently, the themes of faith, hope, and love are beautifully interwoven throughout Scripture. That is why I have chosen to develop this collection of "sermon starters" around these three related subject areas. I hope they will stimulate pastors, teachers, and other communicators to go back to the Word of God to discover God's divine teaching concerning these vital areas of the Christian life.

AL BRYANT

SCRIPTURE INDEX

Joshua
14:12 23

Psalms
42:5 . . . . . . 36, 38
42:11 36

Proverbs
3:5–6 27

Hosea
11:4 47

Jonah
2:7 39

Micah
7:7 10

Matthew
15:28 25

Mark
5:36 22

Luke
1:4 21
5:12 20

10:27 48
12:32 18
17:5 25

John
3:16 58
12:3 52
13:34 53
13:35 54
15:12 49

Acts
2:40 26
27:22, 25 40

Romans
5 15
10:10 16
12:21 51
13:8 51

1 Corinthians
1:7 56
12:26 50
13:13 9

2 Corinthians
5:7 27

5:14 58

Ephesians
2:12 45

2 Timothy
1:12 62

Hebrews
11:1 12
11:8 30
13:7 19

1 Peter
1:9 32
1:21 11
3:15 41
4:8 63

1 John
3:1 56
4:7–8 54
4:8 60
5:4 33

Revelation
2:10 31

FAITH, HOPE, AND LOVE

Now abideth faith, hope, and love (1 Cor. 13:13).

A pastor sought to comfort a young dying doctor in the north of England by telling him, "The past is all answered for in the death of Christ's atonement; the present is all provided for in Christ's shepherd care; and the future is all secured in Christ's coming glory."

The three graces, faith, love, and hope, have their own outlook and emphasis.

I. Faith's witness is, "He bore my sins in His own body on the tree" (1 Peter 2:24); love's witness is, "I love Him because He first loved me" (1 John 4:19); hope's witness is, "I shall be satisfied when I awake in His likeness" (Ps. 17:15).

II. Faith sings, "He loved me and gave Himself for me" (Gal. 2:20); love sings, "Having loved His own, He loves them to the uttermost" (John 13:1); hope sings, "Kept by the power of God, unto the salvation ready to be revealed" (1 Peter 1:5).

III. Faith emphasizes the death of Christ as the starting point of the Christian life, "I declared unto you first of all, Christ died" (1 Cor. 15:3). Love emphasizes the life of Christ in His resurrection power as the lifting power to the higher life, "That I may know Him and the power of His resurrection" (Phil. 3:10). Hope emphasizes the kinship of Christ and anticipates His Kingly glory by knowing His Kingly sway in the heart now. "Sanctify Christ as Lord in the heart" (1 Peter 3:15 RV).

F. E. Marsh

THREE SUPREME RESOLUTIONS
FOR THE NEW YEAR

Therefore I will look unto the Lord; I will wait for the God of my salvation; my God will hear me (Mic. 7:7).

These are the words of one who was saddened and chafed and perplexed. The depravities of society, its treacheries, its selfishness, its furious lust, overpowered all faith but faith in God. It compelled, through a terrible discipline, and yet a gracious one, to that Christlike attitude of perfect resignation, and perfect devotion, and perfect hope depicted by the text.

I.   **The resolution of faith.** "I will look unto the Lord." The prophet's determination was evidently the result of eminent wisdom and prompt decision of character. Man's look. God's look.
     A. The promises encourage me.
     B. Experience teaches me.
     C. The Lord commands me.
     D. The engagement will comfort me.

II. **The resolution of patience.** "I will wait for the God of my salvation." The patient exercise of hope.
     A. "I will wait," for His time is best.
     B. "I will wait," for His blessing is worth waiting for.
     C. "I will wait," for I shall not be disappointed.

III. **The confidence of hope.** "My God will hear me."
     A. Though my cry be feeble and my faith weak, "my God will hear me."
     B. Though my request be great, "my God will hear me."
     C. Though others disdain me, "my God will hear me." For He is near. The prophet's communion was with God. His expectation was from God. Looking to God and waiting for God. Here is the great ground for encouragement. In the same faith let us make our new year resolutions, and our renewed resolutions all the years through.

Selected

THE OBJECT OF OUR FAITH AND HOPE

That your faith and hope might be in God (1 Peter 1:21).

Faith trusts—hope expects. Faith accepts the testimony—hope expects the blessing. We first believe, and then hope. Faith and hope are welded links of the same chain, and the end of the chain holds on to Christ crucified, and Christ risen again. Now our faith and hope should not be,

I. In ourselves.

Our righteousness is as filthy rags. Our desert, death. Our estate, pollution. Our condition, utter moral insolvency.

II. In our fellow creatures.

Not in patriarchs—nor Moses—nor the prophets—nor apostles—nor martyrs—nor priests—nor saints, living or dead—nor in the Virgin Mary.

III. In angels.

We may hail them as friends. Emulate their goodness. Rejoice in their ministrations—but they are not mediators, nor objects of faith and hope.

IV. But our faith and hope should be in God.

A. In the *Father*—the source and fountain of all goodness and mercy.

B. In the *Son of God*—the one mediator, sacrifice, and only Savior.

C. In the *Holy Spirit of God*—the fountain of grace the light—the truth and solace of our souls.

Application:

1. To avoid *false trusts* and illusive confidences.

2. Learn that *God only* is the *living* fountain of waters. All else cisterns, broken cisterns.

3. Learn how *needful* is *self-examination*. Do we really, consciously believe and hope in God? Have we the evidence in our hearts, and the fruit thereof in our lives? Let us sing—

Now I have found the ground wherein
Sure my soul's anchor may remain.

Jabez Burns

CHARACTERISTICS OF FAITH

Hebrews 11:1

Hope of faith (Gal. 5:5).
Joy of faith (Phil. 1:25).
Confidence of faith (Eph. 3:12).
Boldness in speaking (2 Cor. 4:13).
Peace (Rom. 15:13).
Rest (Heb. 4:3).
Fight of faith (1 Tim. 6:12).
Believers live by faith (Heb. 2:4).
Believers stand by faith (2 Cor. 1:24).
Believers walk by faith (2 Cor. 5:7).
Believers resist the Devil (1 Peter 5:9).
Believers overcome the world (1 John 5:4).
Believers obtain a good report (Heb. 11:39).
Believers overcome difficulties (Heb. 11:33).
Believers die in faith (Heb. 11:13).
We are saved by faith (Acts 16:31).
We get remission of sins (Rom. 3:25).
We are adopted by faith (Gal. 3:26).
We are justified by faith (Rom. 5:1).
We are sanctified by faith (Acts 26:18).
We are purified by faith (Acts 15:9).
We are edified by faith (1 Tim. 1:4).
We are kept by faith (1 Peter 1:5).
We have access to God by faith (Rom. 5:2).
We inherit the promises (Heb. 6:12).
Saints should be sincere (1 Tim. 1:5).
Saints should abound (2 Cor. 8:7).
Saints should continue (Acts 2:22).
Saints should be strong in faith (Rom. 4:20–21).

Selected

FAITH IN EXERCISE

Living (Gal. 2:20).
Obeying (Rom. 16:26).
Walking (2 Cor. 5:7).
Working (1 Thess. 1:3).
Praying (James 5:15).
Enduring (1 Peter 1:7).
Fighting (1 Tim. 6:12).

Selected

TRUE FAITH AND ITS FRUITS

The man believed the word that Jesus had spoken unto him (John 4:50).

If thou believest with all thine heart (Acts 8:37).

Lord, I believe; help Thou mine unbelief (Mark 9:24).

A great number believed and turned unto the Lord (Acts 11:21).

Whosoever believeth that Jesus is the Christ, is born of God (1 John 5:1).

Who is he that overcometh the world, but he that believeth that Jesus is the Son of God (1 John 5:5).

As many as received Him, to them gave He power to become the sons of God, even to them that believe on His name (John 1:12).

Whosoever believeth in Him shall receive remission of sins (Acts 10:43).

He that cometh to Me shall never hunger; and He that believeth on Me shall never thirst (John 6:35).

We should be to the praise of His glory, who first trusted in Christ (Eph. 1:12).

In whom ye also trusted, after that ye heard the word of truth, the gospel of your salvation: in whom also after that ye believed, ye were sealed with that Holy Spirit of promise (Eph. 1:13).

The multitude of them that believed were of one heart and of one soul (Acts 4:32).

They which have believed in God should be careful to maintain good works (Titus 3:8).

Believe on the Lord Jesus Christ, and thou shalt be saved (Acts 16:31).

We are not of them who draw back unto perdition; but of them that believe to the saving of the soul (Heb. 10:39).

God so loved the world, that He gave His only begotten Son, that whosoever believeth in Him should not perish, but have everlasting life (John 3:16).

He that believeth on the Son hath everlasting life (John 3:36).

Whosoever believeth in Me shall never die (John 11:26).

He that believeth on the Son of God hath the witness in himself (1 John 5:10).

I know whom I have believed, and am persuaded that he is able to keep that which I have committed unto him against that day (2 Tim. 1:12).

We which have believed do enter into rest (Heb. 4:3).

Believing, ye rejoice with joy unspeakable and full of glory (1 Peter 1:8).

Receiving the end of your faith, even the salvation of your souls (1 Peter 1:9).

Selected

WHAT WE GAIN BY FAITH

Pardon (Acts 10:43).
Peace with God (Rom. 5:1).
Eternal Life (John 3:36).
The Holy Spirit (John 7:39).
Sonship (Gal. 3:26).
Heirship (Rom. 8:17).

Selected

WHAT WE DO BY FAITH

We live (Rom. 1:17).
We stand (2 Cor. 1:24).
We walk (2 Cor. 5:7).
We fight (1 Tim. 6:52).
We overcome (1 John 5:4).

Selected

FAITH

Faith's key unlocks the treasury of *grace*, and gives us fourteen things of priceless value, as seen in Romans 5:

1. The Holy Spirit (v. 5).
2. The love of God in our hearts (v. 5).
3. Atonement (v. 11).
4. Reconciliation to God (v. 10).
5. Justification now by His blood (v. 9).
6. Salvation from wrath. Salvation by His life (v. 9).
7. Abundance of grace (v. 17).
8. Gift of righteousness (v. 17).
9. Access to God (v. 2).
10. Stand (v. 2).
11. Peace with God (v. 1).
12. Joy in God (v. 11).
13. Rejoicing in hope (v. 2).
14. Reign in life (v. 17).

Selected

ASSURANCE OF FAITH

John 5:24; 6:47; 10:28
Romans 8:1
Philippians 1:6
Ephesians 2:6
2 Timothy 1:12
1 John 2:25
Hebrews 13:5

FACTS ABOUT FAITH

By faith we live (Rom. 1:17).
By faith we stand (2 Cor. 1:24).
By faith we walk (2 Cor. 5:7).
By faith we fight (1 Tim. 6:52).
By faith we overcome (1 John 5:4).
By faith we are justified (Rom. 3:28).
By faith we are made children of God (Gal. 3:26).
By faith we are sanctified (Acts 26:18).
By faith we have access (Rom. 5:2; Eph. 3:12).
Faith purifies the heart (Acts 15:9).
Without faith we cannot please God (Heb. 11:6).

Selected

THE BELIEVER'S GROWTH IN FAITH

With the heart man believeth unto righteousness (Rom. 10:10).

We partially know about God by thinking; we fully know Him only by believing. Theories will change, but heart experiences of the divine presence in the soul are the same as when God walked with Adam in Eden. The feelings of sin and sorrow, of joy and peace, are common to all ages, and all hearts.

I. There can be no evolution in the nature of love and faith. The only change may be in the evermore increasing volume. The Lord's Prayer is hallowed for the heart. God's love shed abroad in the heart makes all Christians one in Him.

An American who met a heathen convert in India saw the light of peace and joy on his face. They recognized each other as followers of Jesus, but they could not convey by words the likeness of their experience, except that there are two words which are the same in all languages; so one said "Amen" and the other, "Hallelujah!" Thus a single word may express volumes of heart experience, because it awakens similar feelings in consciousness.

II. While the mind is often lost in the labyrinths of speculation, the heart, through the telescope of faith, sees the

Father's home a palace of splendor at the end of the way, and feels the joy unspeakable and full of glory.

III. The way of the doubter is hard and gloomy, but the way of faith is the path of hope and leads to everlasting triumph.

Selected

A DEFINITION OF FAITH

I. What is faith? (John 14:1; Rom. 10:6–10; 2 Cor. 5:7; Heb. 11:1–2).

II. The truth to be believed (Ps. 27:13; Matt. 9:28–30; Mark 11:24; Heb. 11:3).

III. The aim of faith (Heb. 2:6; John 3:16; 2 Cor. 1:24; 1 Tim. 1:5).

IV. The results of faith (Acts 10:43; Rom. 10:9–11; Gal. 2:20; Eph. 3:12).

V. The testing of faith (Gen. 22:15–18; John 11:25–27; James 1:3; 1 Peter 1:7).

VI. The power of faith (Matt. 9:28–30; Mark 9:23; Eph. 6:16; James 5:15).

VII. From faith to fruition (Rom. 4:3; Heb. 4:3; James 2:17; 1 John 5:4).

J. H. Vincent

FEAR AND FAITH

Fear not, little flock; for it is your Father's good pleasure to give you the kingdom (Luke 12:32).

These words were spoken as a command by the Master to those of His early followers who were beset by foes.

I. Jesus knew the ill effects of fear—that distemper of the soul. He knew that it could be overcome only by belief, strong and clean, in the God who rules above our petty cares and vicissitudes.

II. How can we banish fear from our lives—fear of failure, fear of poverty, fear of loneliness, and many an unspoken dread that keeps our spirits in bondage?

A. First, let us drag our fears out into the open and face them boldly. Many a trouble vanishes in the sunlight. Fears thrive in darkness or half darkness. Our fears lie often in our subconscious and dog us like shadows. To tell our fears, to analyze them, to find out their source, is to half destroy them.

B. Second, let us believe in God—His promises and His love and His desire to give us good and not bad things. Fear is unbelief. Cultivate belief in God's men and women and in God's world; get the habit of believing in people, in seeing the good and in overlooking the evil. Remember that if you really want to believe in men and in God, you will slowly but surely get the habit of faith. Browning says: "If you desire faith, then you've faith enough."

III. But faith is a moving, active thing. It is more than desire; it needs the act of the will. Let me try today believing in a friendly universe. I will be positive and not negative. I will be a believer and not a cynic. Faith grows, and, growing, crowds out fear.

Selected

FAITH'S LANGUAGE

Whose faith follow (Heb. 13:7).

It is a good thing to so work that we are willing to have the work of our hands established. Spurgeon once said: "My brother said to me the other day what Charles Wesley said to John Wesley, 'Brother, our people die well!' I answered, 'Assuredly they do!' I have never been to the sickbed of any of our people without feeling strengthened in faith. In the sight of their glorious confidence, I could sooner battle with the whole earth and kick it before me like a football, than have a doubt in my mind about the Gospel of our Lord. They die gloriously. I saw, last week, a dear sister with cancer just under her eye. How did I find her? Was she lamenting her hard fate? By no means; she was happy, calm, joyful, in bright expectation of seeing the face of the King in His beauty. I talked with a tradesman who fell asleep not long ago, and I said, 'You seem to have no fears ?' 'No,' he said, 'how can I have any? You have not taught us what will make us fear. How can I be afraid to die, since I have fed these thirty years on the strong meat of the kingdom of God? I know whom I have believed.' I had a heavenly time with him. I cannot use a lower word. He exhibited a holy mirth in the expectation of a speedy removal to the better world. Now, dear brethren, thrice happy shall we be, if we can say, in the last hour, 'I have not shunned to declare the whole counsel of God.'"

The testimony of those who have passed on in the faith of Christ is always inspiring and faith-begetting. The men of faith have always been positive in their testimonies.

    I.   **Job could say, "I know that my Redeemer liveth (Job 19:25).**

    II.   **Paul affirmed, "I know whom I have believed" (2 Tim. 1:12).**

    III.   **John proclaimed, "We know we have passed from death to life" (1 John 3:14).**

    IV.   **Isaiah witnessed, "Behold, God is my Salvation" (Isa. 12:2).**

    V.   **Peter wrote, "Who His own Self bare our sins on the tree" (1 Peter 2:24).**

VI. David sang, "The Lord is my Rock and Fortress" (Ps. 18:2).

VII. Habakkuk joyously exclaimed, "The Lord God is my Strength" (Hab. 3:19).

F. E. Marsh

RESPONSIVENESS OF THE LORD TO FAITH

Thou wilt (Luke 5:12).

Evangelist Gipsy Smith once related how his daughter commenced a meeting for young people, and one night there appeared a ragged urchin, who had a pair of pants whose legs were not of corresponding size, and out of which was hanging part of another garment called a "shirt." The boy's hair was like an electrified haystack, and his face was as black as a coal-miner's. It was the custom of the class, when the roll was called, for each member to repeat a text. When each member had done this, "Zillah" (Miss Smith) turned to the black-faced boy and said, "Of course, my boy, you not being in the habit of attending our class, have not a text."

"Ain't I, though; I 'ave."

"Well, we shall be glad to hear it."

Remember the boy's face was black—very black. Lifting up his grimy face to the teacher's, and his black eyes twinkling, he said: "Lord, if Thou wilt, Thou canst make me clean."

The following "Thou wilt's" in the Psalms reveal the expectancy of faith as confirmation of the leper's cry.

I. **Blessing**—"For Thou, Lord, wilt bless the righteous" (Ps. 5:12). The blessings of forgiveness, peace, deliverance, power, holiness, joy, alone can come from Him.

II. **Protection**—"O Lord, with favor Thou wilt compass him as with a shield" (Ps. 5:12). He surrounds as a wall of fire, as an army, as a hedge, as mountains around a city, as a shield, and as a fortress.

III. **Revelation**—"Thou wilt show me the path of life" (Ps. 16:11). He will reveal the way out of difficulty, doubt, despair, danger and death.

IV. **Confidence**—"Thou wilt hear me" (Ps. 17:6). To those who truly pray, the Lord has always an answer. He who knocks at heaven's gate always finds an open door.

V. **Illumination**—"Thou wilt light my candle" (Ps. 18:28). He will not leave us in the dark, and He will also supply the "lamp" (RV) of our being with the oil of the Spirit.

VI. **Comfort**—"Thou wilt make all his bed in his sickness " (Ps. 41:3). The Lord as the Bed-maker will surely supply the feathery bed of His love, the soft pillow of peace, the blankets of comfort, and the eiderdown of cover-all.

VII. **Revival**—"Wilt Thou not revive us again?" (Ps. 95:6). Of course, He will. There is no need to ask the question when He is ready to answer every question.

F. E. Marsh

CERTAINTIES OF THE FAITH

The certainty of those things (Luke 1:4).

One, in writing on the trend of the times, says: "In the intellectual sphere, Christianity in its dogmatic position has been badly shaken by destructive and disruptive criticism from all sides; the result is that, save in the Roman Catholic Church (which at least knows where it stands, and therefore keeps going as a vital religious institution), there is something of a theological panic in all the churches. There is a chaos of conflicting opinions on all doctrinal points, and some modern divines are out to 'save' Christianity by explaining it away."

The same journalist remarks:

"Small wonder that the layman, who can obtain no clear teaching on the things that puzzle him, abandons institutional religion altogether, and carries on as best he can."

May we not remind the writer, that if he will but follow the teaching of Christ, he will find His teaching is clear and satisfying. He will find it in the following seven great and glorious facts.

I. **The fact of God's love,** in Christ's assurance, "For God so loved the world, that He gave His only-begotten Son" (John 3:16).

II. **The fact of promised rest,** in Christ's loving invitation, "Come unto Me, all ye that labor and are heavy laden, and I will give you rest" (Matt. 11:28).

III. **The fact of atonement for sin,** in Christ's emphatic Word, "The Son of Man came not to be ministered unto, but to minister, and to give His life a ransom for many" (Matt. 20:28).

IV. **The fact of god's paternal care,** in Christ's hallowed words, "Your Father knoweth what things ye have need of" (Matt. 6:32).

V. **The fact of the true secret of life,** in His Example of serving others, finding the true life in losing the soulish one (John 12:24–26).

VI. **The fact of true relationship in life,** to the Divine and the human, in doing the will of God (Matt. 12:50).

VII. **The fact of Christ's soul-heartening promise for the future,** that He will come again, and receive us to Himself (John 14:3).

F. E. Marsh

THE FAITH THAT TRANSFORMS THE LIFE

Only believe (Mark 5:36).

For nearly two thousand years people have looked to Christ as their ideal. Many characterizations have been made of His greatness. Some have said that it existed in His obedience, others in His suffering, still others in His friendship for men. Soaring above all these traits, however, and giving point and inspiration to them, was irresistible faith in His divine and omnipotent Father.

I. He believed in God more implicitly than has any other person who has ever lived. This raised Christ above all human circumstances. This determined His Godhood.

To the Master, faith literally could remove mountains, since it was unfettered by doubt. He typified religion as a little child looking up implicitly into his father's face and believing utterly in his parent. The child is not troubled with the shame and sorrow and fears of the universe—he leaves them to his father. These things are not in the child's consciousness; if they come, the confidence the child has in his parent surmounts them. Faith is first and foremost.

II.   Christianity is thus at bottom a great adventure of faith. Faith is the foolishness that, the Scriptures tell us, confounds the wise. The righteous, says Paul, shall live by faith. A Christian is best defined as a believer; a non-Christian as an unbeliever. Christ staked all on this principle, which He uttered to the ruler of the synagogue as a determining factor. His insistent rule of Christian power and success is: "All things are possible to him that believeth."

III.   Do we realize what this means? "All things!" Do we act as though we really believed this first principle of Christianity? In my life this day, let me apply it to something definite. Two thousand years ago the ruler of a Jewish synagogue believed and the seemingly impossible was performed.

Selected

ATTEMPTING HIGH AND HARD THINGS
(Faith in Motion)

Now therefore give me this hill-country (Josh. 14:12 RV).

This is one of the fascinating passages of the Old Testament. It stirs one's imagination and determination to hear Caleb ask Joshua, who was dividing up the land, for a place for strenuous living and work. He might well have pleaded the privilege of preference because of the promise made him years before and, also, because of the infirmities of age. He had every reason to expect something easy. But, instead, he said, "Give me something to do that will require my best."

I.   We respond to that spirit, yet shrink from possessing it. Christianity began with it, and has had it most when it has conquered most. The church has always been at its best when meeting hardship and adversity, and at its worst in comfort and prosperity.

II. The individual Christian life is not fundamentally different. "Now therefore give me this hill-country" where dwell power and health and vision.

III. "As I was in the day that Moses sent me, even so is my strength now. Now, therefore, give me this mountain." Anakims were there. Giants were there. Joshua granted his petition, commended his bravery, applauded his request, and gave him what he asked. He also prayed for him, that he might have good success.

A New England farmer was asked why he did not move to the rich, soft fertile western prairie. He said, "I would hate to put down my spade when it would not strike a stone." That was the spirit of Caleb.

A famous ironworker who had wrought many artistic pieces for Queen Victoria, remarked, "There is a certain satisfaction in taking the crude, refractory metal and hammering it into a thing of grace and beauty."

There is a zest in doing hard things well which the man never tastes who confines himself to easy undertakings. Who save those who have experienced it can understand the satisfaction with which the woodsmen feels his well tempered blade bite deep into the frosty log?

One is almost tempted to reverse Plutarch and read, "Hard things are good." At least we know that if there were no heavy loads, all backs would be flabby.

Selected

INCREASE OF FAITH

And the apostles said unto the Lord, "Increase our faith" (Luke 17:5).

It was a great and good thing the apostles asked.

I. Faith is capable of increase.
A. In the amount of truth it embraces.

B. In the degree of intensity with which it lays hold of its object.

C. In the force with which it works.

II. The increase of faith is desirable.
A. For the sake of our holiness.

B. For the sake of our happiness.

C. For the sake of our usefulness.

III. This increase of faith is to be sought through prayer. "Lord, increase."
A. Our prayer for the increase of faith should be earnest.

B. It should be accompanied with habitual meditation on the object of faith.

C. Our prayer for the increase of faith should be accompanied with avoidance of everything that tends to impair the strength of faith.

GREAT FAITH

Matthew 15:28

I. Great Faith Leads to Great Undertakings.
It was a great undertaking for this woman mentioned in the Scriptures to come to Christ.

II. Great Faith Begets Great Expectations.
She expected the Savior to heal her daughter. We often expect no great results from our labors, because we have not this great faith.

III. Great Faith Awakens Great Earnestness.
She cried, and fell at His feet and worshiped Him. Look at the earnestness of Knox, Luther, Wesley, etc. They had great faith.

IV. Great Faith Conquers Great Difficulties.

First it is said, "He answered her not a word." But she kept on. Next He said He was not sent but to the lost sheep of the house of Israel. Still she was not discouraged. Next He said, "It was not meet to take the children's bread and cast it to the dogs." She answered, "Truth O Lord". . . What difficulties have not been overcome by people of undaunted courage and faith!

V. Great Faith Achieves Great Victories.

"Be it unto thee even as thou wilt," and her daughter was made whole (Matt. 17:20; Mark 9:23; Heb. 11:30–40).

100 Sermon Outlines

HAVING GOALS (Faith in Action)

Save yourselves from this untoward generation (Acts 2:40).

The word "untoward" is the opposite of toward. When one goes toward a place one is moving in the direction of that place.

I. Untoward movement is movement that is not getting anywhere. It may be movement in a circle, merry-go-round movement. It may be the natural movement of a man that is lost.

II. A whole generation may be going in circles. One must save one's self from it to get ahead of it. The drag of the crowd is terrific. The circle of conformity is deadly. Jesus might have slipped into the Pharisee's circle. Paul did for a time move in that circle, but he broke from it.

III. The first step in breaking from a get-nowhere generation is to catch sight of a goal. Such a goal Jesus can give us. Jesus can give an objective, an objective embedded in the heart of reality. Let's go. Let's not merely go places. Let's go some place. There is such a goal and one can come at it. That is what faith in Christ can do for us. We know where we are going and we are on the way.

M. K. W. Heicher

THE HIGHER WISDOM (Faith)

Trust in the Lord with all thine heart; and lean not unto thine own understanding. In all thy ways acknowledge him, and he shall direct thy paths (Prov. 3:5–6).

Introduction:

The fallibility of our own understanding, subject to errors of judgment, warped by our prejudices, blinded by our sins.

I. The Lord directs our paths by giving us clearer perceptions—a higher "common sense."

II. He directs our paths by modifying our values. First things are put first.

III. He directs our paths by giving us a higher knowledge of His purposes.

IV. He directs our paths by revealing Christ as "the Way, the Truth, the Life."

To attain this higher wisdom:

1. Trust in the Lord.

2. Acknowledge Him in all your ways.

M. K. W. Heicher

FAITH'S WALK

We walk by faith, not by appearance (2 Cor. 5:7).

To delight in the Lord means wholehearted obedience to Him; and this makes Him to delight in us. To love Him in our obedience is to find His love our comfort.

John Wesley writes in his diary: "My brother Charles among the difficulties of our early ministry used to say, 'If the Lord would give me wings I would fly.' I used to answer, 'If the Lord bids me fly I would trust Him for the wings.'" All God bids us do, He virtually promises to help us do.

I. The way of faith is not the way of sight. That is, it is not the looking for *evidences*, either in our own feeling, or in the circumstances that attend us. True faith does not ask for these things. It rests on something altogether apart from them.

II. **The way of faith is not the way of effort.** That is, when we are trusting another to do a thing for us, we have ceased to try to do it for ourselves, and real faith is confidence in God that He is working in our behalf. So, instead of bringing worry and effort into our hearts, it brings rest.

III. **The way of faith is the way of reliance upon the Character and Promise of Another—upon God and His Word.** Faith looks to God to work as He has said He would; and refuses to undertake for itself, except to fulfill those conditions that God may have laid down with His promise. Indeed, the largest part of faith's struggle, often, is to *keep from interfering* on its own behalf—to *keep from helping God out*, as it were. Unbelief cannot and will not wait for God to work, but must rush ahead to help itself. Thus it fails to receive from God; for "He works for him that *waits for Him*" (Isa. 44:4 RV). Faith, on the contrary, is willing to endure trial, and to wait long, if need be, until God is ready to interpose on its behalf. It knows that "He is faithful who has promised," and "though the vision tarry, it will wait for it, for it will surely come."

A great part of faith's work, therefore, is *fighting unbelief, refusing* to look at those things that dishearten, and destroy confidence. Satan is ever ready with temptations to doubt. Often, too, the circumstances about us are such as would in themselves utterly discourage us. God often "waits to be gracious" until our self-hopes and efforts are done. He is the real faith—*to hold on*, in the midst of these untoward things, until, in His good time, *God works*.

IV. **Faith's victory consists in holding fast to God's promise until He sends help.** Faith has *all things* promised to her (Mark 9:23). If she will but *stand*, and *trust* God and *wait*, she can have anything she needs or asks. Let her but refuse *to doubt*, refuse to move, or *question*, or give back in any wise, and the triumph will surely be hers, in due season.

V. **The way of faith is God's way with His people.** He has no other. "*Without* faith it is *impossible* to be well-pleasing unto Him" (Heb. 11:6).

F. E. Marsh

ON FAITH AND FAITHFULNESS

There is nothing so much appreciated by our Lord as faithfulness.

I. **Faithfulness is the mark of stewardship, for a steward must be "found *faithful*" (1 Cor. 4:2).**

II. **Faithfulness is the stamp of a genuine believer—"What part hath he that *believeth* with an infidel?" (2 Cor. 6:15).**

III. **Faithfulness is the qualification of a true minister—"a *faithful* minister of Christ" (Col. 1:7; 4:7, 9).**

IV. **Faithfulness is the summary of the Christian life—"He that is *faithful* in that which is least is *faithful* also in much" (Luke 16:10).**

V. **Faithfulness is the certificate to trustworthiness in the things of God—"If you have judged me *faithful*" (Acts 16:15); "commit to *faithful* men" (2 Tim. 2:2; 1 Tim. 3:2).**

VI. **Faithfulness is the fulfillment of the Lord's command—"Be thou *faithful*" (Rev. 2:10).**

VII. **Faithfulness always calls forth the Lord's commendation—"Well done, good and *faithful* servant" (Matt. 25:21, 23; Luke 19:17; Gal. 2:9; Eph. 6:21; Col. 4:9; 1 Tim. 1:12; Heb. 3:2; 1 Peter 5:12; 3 John 5; Rev. 2:13).**

To truly recognize the faithfulness of our Lord is to respond to Him in faithfulness. Faith feeds upon God's faithfulness, and becomes faithful and full.

F. E. Marsh

FAITH—LIFE'S GREATEST VENTURE

By faith Abraham went forth, not knowing whither he went (Heb. 11:8).

Faith is more than a mental conclusion; it involves decisions and movement—an active will.

1. It is here that many people fail to recognize the vital difference between a theological creed and a religious life, between a mental assent and a consent of the will, between belief and faith. The difference is something like the difference between the legislative and administrative functions in the national government. Administration is law in action. The vital element in faith is movement of the will, adventuring forth.

2. And so the real proofs in spiritual things can only be found in experience. A man ventures forth at the bidding of the Lord, and as he goes along he begins to have "the evidence of things not seen."

3. But note that this belief is walking, not merely talking; it is to this kind of valorous action that the light of life is promised. The vital proofs are given in experience. "It came to pass that as he went he received his sight." We must not wait for our proofs; we must go forth to meet them.

4. And thus it is that the Christian life, because it is a splendid venture, is also a bracing exploration and a magnificent discovery. It is life's greatest "find," compared with which everything else is as nothing, for it is "the Pearl of Great Price."

Selected

FAITH NOT FEAR

Fear not the things which thou art about to suffer (Rev. 2:10 RV).

Introduction:

The book of Revelation helped the Christians of the early church to fight the Battle of Morale. To do this:

I. Seek sound morality.

Seek moral soundness because the crisis or ordeal increases moral momentum. How men bear up in the ordeal depends largely upon where they really stood when they went in. Seek sound morality because the final victory is moral victory.

II. Seek firm faith (read Rev. 2:13).

By faith one knows that God is working out His purposes, that He is not removed from one's sufferings. Faith is the victory that overcomes.

III. Seek steadfast endurance.

"Hold that line!" "They shall not pass!" "Be ye faithful unto death and I will give thee the crown of life." The faithfulness of man is climaxed by the faithfulness of God.

IV. Seek genuine humility.

Humility before God, not just a "humility" before facts and circumstances, before Powers and Dominions, before men and human authorities.

M. K. W. Heicher

THE END OF FAITH

Receiving the end of your faith, even the salvation of your souls
(1 Peter 1:9).

Without faith it is impossible to please God. Faith is essential to pardon, holiness, eternal life.

I.   The faith of the text—"Your faith."
So it is clear that this faith,

A. Is evangelical. Faith in the Lord Jesus Christ and in the Gospel of salvation.

B. It is saving. The end, the salvation of your souls. Much that is called faith is simply an acceptance of Scripture inspiration and authority, but recognizes no personal sinfulness, penalty or peril. Saving faith realizes guilt, deplores it, confesses it, and finds salvation in the person and work of the Lord Jesus Christ.

C. It is personal—"your faith." Not the creed of a sect, or the belief of a multitude, but the faith wrought in your heart, and exercised consciously in the Son of God.

Now, notice,

II.   The receptivity of this faith.
"The salvation of your souls." This "receptivity" includes,

A. Justification and the remission of sins.

B. Acceptance with God.

C. Peace and joy in the Holy Ghost.

D. A renewed heart.

E. A good hope of immortality and eternal life, Now salvation includes these, all these, and nothing less.

III.   Observe:

A. This salvation is God's free gift.

B. The result of Christ's offices and work.

C. Imparted by the Holy Spirit—and only,

D. Realizable by faith. Unbelief shuts the eye—closes the ear—hardens the heart—and refuses the mercy of heaven. Faith looks to the Savior, and in Him finds the salvation.

Jabez Burns

YOUR FAITH

1. **Basis** of Faith. "Faith cometh by hearing, and hearing by the Word of God" (Rom. 10:17).

2. **Object** of Faith. "I believe God" (Acts 27:25).

3. **Secret** of Faith. "I live by the faith of the Son of God" (Gal. 2:20).

4. **Trial** of Faith. "The trial of your faith" (1 Peter 1:7).

5. **Power** of Faith. "Fruit of the Spirit . . . faith" (Gal. 5:22).

6. **Prayer** of Faith. "The prayer of faith shall save the sick" (James 5:15).

7. **Victory** of Faith. "This is the victory that overcometh the world, even our faith" (1 John 5:4).

F. E. Marsh

VICTORIOUS FAITH

For whatsoever is born of God overcometh the world: and this is the victory that overcometh the world, even our faith" (1 John 5:4).

I. The Conquest Itself: "Overcometh the world."

A. We break loose from the world's customs.

B. We maintain our freedom to obey a higher Master in all things. We are not enslaved by dread of poverty, greed of riches, official command, personal ambition, love of honor, fear of shame, or force of numbers.

C. We are above the world's authority. Its ancient customs or novel edicts are for its own children: we do not own it as a ruler, or as a judge,

D. We are above its religion. We gather our religion from God and His Word, not from human sources.

As one in whom this conquest was seen, read the story of Abraham. Think of him in connection with his quitting home, his lonely wanderings, his conduct toward Lot, Sodom and her king, Isaac, etc.

II. The Conquering Nature: "Whatsoever is born of God."

A. This nature alone will undertake the contest with the world.

B. This nature alone can continue it. All else wearies in the fray. This nature is born to conquer, God is the Lord, and that which is born of Him is royal and ruling.

III. The Conquering Weapon: "Even our faith."

We are enabled to be conquerors through regarding—

A. The unseen reward which awaits us.

B. The unseen presence which surrounds us. God and a cloud of witnesses hold us in full survey.

C. The mystic union to Christ which grace has wrought in us. Resting in Jesus we overcome the world.

IV. The Speciality of It: "This is *the* victory."

A. For salvation, finding the rest of faith.

B. For imitation, finding the wisdom of Jesus, the Son of God.

C. For consolation, seeing victory secured to us in Jesus,
Behold your conflict—born to battle.
Behold your triumph—bound to conquer.

When a traveler was asked whether he did not admire the admirable structure of some stately building, "No," said he, "*for I have been at Rome, where better are to be seen every day.*" O believer, if the world tempt you with rare sights and curious prospects, you may well scorn them, having been, by contemplation, in heaven, and being able, by faith, to see infinitely better delights every hour of the day! "This is the victory that overcometh the world, even our faith."
—Feathers for Arrows

The believer not only overcomes the world in its deformities, but in its seeming excellencies. Not in the way that Alexander and other conquerors overcame it, but in a much nobler way; for they, so far from overcoming the world, were slaves to the world. The man who puts ten thousand other men to death does not overcome the world.

The true conqueror is he who can say, with Paul, "Thanks be to God, who giveth us the victory through our Lord Jesus Christ," and, "Who shall separate us from the love of Christ? Shall tribulation?" etc. "Nay, in all these things we are more than conquerors, through him that loved us." Such a one has recourse, by faith, to an infallible standard—the Word of God: indeed, there is no other. He detects the world, and will not be imposed upon by it. When he is tempted to take the world's good things as his portion, he rejects them; because he has something better in hand.

Thus, faith in Christ overcomes the corrupt influence, the inordinate love, the slavish fear, the idolatry, the friendship, the false wisdom, and the maxims of the world: it overcomes not only the folly, but the very religion of the world, as far as it is a false religion.
—RICHARD CECIL

It is asserted of this elegant creature (the Bird of Paradise) that it always flies against the wind; as, otherwise, its beautiful, but delicate plumage would be ruffled and spoiled. Those only are the Birds of Paradise, in a spiritual sense, who make good their way against the wind of worldliness; a wind always blowing in an opposite direction to that of heaven.   —J. D. HULL

Spurgeon

THE CHRISTIAN'S HOPE

Hope thou in God (Ps. 42:5).

Hope is an essential. More so in seasons of darkness, depression, weakness.

I. **The thing that is here urged—"hope."** That is, expect all needful future good of every kind. Both in religious work and enjoyment. There is no limit to the region of hope.

II. **The object of hope is presented—"in God."** Not in self, not in men, but in God. He is the "God of hope." Christ, the Son, who is our hope. The Holy Spirit is the inspirer and sustainer of hope.

III. **What are some of the various phases of hope?** Similitudes are employed. "Anchor of the soul," in storms and perils. "Light of the soul," in darkness.

IV. **Consider some of the many reasons for this hope.**
   A. God's ability and all-sufficiency.
   B. His willingness to do all we need.
   C. His changeless love—a great assurance and source of hope.
   D. His precious promises—many, ample, sure. This hope in God is an imperative, glorious privilege, and an unspeakable duty and joy. "Hope thou in God!"

CHEER UP!

Why art thou cast down, O my soul? And why art thou disquieted within me? Hope thou in God: for I shall yet praise him, who is the health of my countenance, and my God (Ps. 42:11).

I. **The causes of spiritual despondency.**
   A. The burden of sin.
   B. The wickedness of the world.
   C. Earthly misfortunes.
   D. Bereavements.

II. The cure of despondency.
A. A present trust in God.
B. A confident look to the future. Who's in charge?

III. The reasons for trust in God!
A. His present goodness to us.
B. His revealed relation to us.

THE HOPE OF THE GOSPEL

1. A Good Hope (2 Thess. 2:16)

2. A Blessed Hope (Titus 2:13)

3. A Joyful Hope (Heb. 3:6; Rom. 5:3)

4. A Sure and Certain Hope (Heb. 6:18)

5. A Lively or Living Hope (1 Peter 1:3)

6. A Saving Hope (Rom. 8:24)

7. A Glorious Hope (Col. 1:27)

8. A Purifying Hope (1 John 3:3)

Selected

THE SAINT'S HOPE

Hope thou in God (Ps. 42:5).

Hope is ever essential. More so in seasons of darkness and depression and weakness. See context.

I. What Is Urged in the Text—"Hope."

That is, expect all needful future good of every kind, and for religious work and enjoyment. No limit to the region of hope.

II. The Object of Hope Is Presented—"In God."

Not in self or men or angels, but in God. In the Father, the "God of hope." In Christ, the Son, who is our hope. In the blessed Spirit, the inspirer and sustainer of hope.

Notice,

III. The Various Phases of Hope.

A. With God's people—all—of every name (Rom. 12:18).

B. With all men.

C. Even with your enemies (5:20). Peace includes all good—God's blessing.

IV. Its Multiplication—"be multiplied."

A. In your own *experience* of it. Deeper, fuller, daily, etc.

B. In your *homes*. Dwellings of peace.

C. In your *religious circles*. Meetings, labors, etc. Church associations.

D. In your *neighborhoods*.

E. In your *nation*. All classes—orders.

F. In the *world*. All lands. Wars cease—brotherly love binds all in one girdle of amity and goodwill (Luke 2:14).

Now notice,

V. Its Desirability.

No personal happiness without the Divine peace—no church prosperity without the spirit of peace—no national progress without it—it is good for all—the laborer and the employer—the rich and the poor—the ruler and the subject. The world's blessedness depends on it.

Now this multiplied peace is,

A. One of the *distinct features* of the Gospel dispensation (Psalm 72). Prince of peace, etc.

B. Of the *prophecies* and *promises* (Micah 4:1). Messiah shall make wars to cease to the ends of the world (Psalm 72).

C. This *peace* of the spirit we must *cultivate*. "As much as lieth in you . . ." "Follow peace" with all men.

D. *Prayer* should ever be *presented*, for it. Similitudes are employed. The anchor of the soul, in storms and perils. The light of the soul in darkness. The elasticity of the soul midst renewed trials.

VI. The Many Reasons for This Hope.
A. God's ability and all-sufficiency.
B. His willingness to do all we need.
C. God's changeless love.
D. God's sworn covenant.
E. God's provided sacrifice.
F. God's precious promises.
G. The Holy Spirit's work in us—for us. This hope in God is an imperative, glorious privilege, and an unspeakable duty and joy.

Jabez Burns

THE REALITY OF HOPE

When my soul fainted within me I remembered the Lord (Jonah 2:7).

The story of Jonah is a lesson in the reality of hope.

I. A prodding shipmaster stirred up Jonah's sleeping conscience.

II. A consciousness of God dawns under various circumstances.

III. Previous experiences with God come to the rescue in a crisis.

IV. Escape mechanisms to save faces are devices to escape truth and reality.

V. God is gracious and patient and guides the disgruntled prophet.

VI. Spiritual retreats are vital soul needs, inspiring and

urgently necessary.

VII.   The prophet knows God better as he reveals him to others.

VIII.   A prodigal prophet turns and tries God's way again.

IX.   God can use any and all situations for His purpose.

X.   Where God and man meet, that is holy ground. And that is our basis for hope.

Selected

CHEERFULNESS

Be of good cheer (Acts 27:22, 25).

Cheerfulness is "living with hope." R. L. Stevenson says of cheerfulness: "Gentleness and cheerfulness . . . they are the perfect duties . . . if your morals make you dreary, depend upon it they are wrong. I do not say give them up, for they may be all you have, but conceal them like a vice, lest they spoil the lives of better and simpler people."

From the above it will be apprehended that cheerfulness is the outcome of a right condition of mind and life. Christ was continually bidding those with whom He came in contact to "be of good cheer," and in each case He had a reason for the "cheer" He enjoined. "Tharseo" comes from "Tharsos." The latter is rendered "courage" (Acts 28:15), hence the former means to have courage. The following instances where "Tharseo" is found suggest that,

I.   Christ Himself is the SOUL of cheerfulness (Acts 23:11).

II.   Forgiveness of sins is the CAUSE of cheerfulness (Matt. 9:2).

III.   Christ's Word is the BASIS of cheerfulness (Mark 6:50).

IV.   WHOLENESS or salvation from sin and disease is the life of cheerfulness (Matt. 9:22).

V.   The calling of Christ is the FEEDER of cheerfulness (Mark 10:49).

VI.   Christ's victory is the PRICE of cheerfulness (John 16:33).

"Tharseo" in each of the above verses is rendered "Be of good cheer" and "Be of good comfort." Christ's cheer is the joy of grace, the comfort of love, the product of holiness, the stimulus of hope, the companion of faith, the contentment of humility, and the courage of confidence.

F. E. Marsh

CHRISTIAN HOPE ACCOUNTED FOR

And be ready always to give an answer to every man that asketh you a reason of the hope that is in you, with meekness and fear (1 Peter 3:15).

True religion must not only be enjoyed, but professed; Christ is to be put on; we are to confess Him before men; our light is to shine for the good of others; we are to be Christ's witnesses and confessors to the people. In doing this, the water of life within us springs up and sends its stream abroad for the good of all around. But more is required of us than even profession; we are to stand forth to vindicate the religion we profess; we are, if necessary, to be disputants in the cause of Christianity; we are to "be ready," etc. Four propositions will bring the subject of the text before us.

I. Christians have a hope within them.

Hope is the expectation of future good; it differs, however, from wishing, or desiring. It is an expectation grounded on what is possible and probable, yea, the certainty of what is satisfactorily established. Christians are the children of hope; unbelievers the slaves of fear. The apostle thus speaks, "Blessed be God," etc. (1 Peter 1:3). The Christian's hope has respect to four things:

A. *An interest in the arrangements of a benignant providence.* The God of providence is the God of grace. Those who are the subjects of His grace are especially interested in a kind and beneficent providence. Of such Christ speaks, when he says, "The very hairs of your head..." "The ways of such are ordered by the Lord." "The Lord keepeth them in the hollow of his hand." "If they commit their way to him..." "No weapon formed against them..."

B. *A full supply of all spiritual blessings.* This supply includes all that they can possibly need in every condition of their pilgrimage to a better world. Their hope embraces that gracious declaration, "My God shall supply..." "The Lord God is a sun..."

C. *A safe and blessed dissolution.* Christians have not always an easy transition; not always a triumphant one; but always a safe one; one of peace and hope. "The righteous hath hope in his death."

D. *A certain glorious resurrection, and eternal life.* The hope of eternal life is the grand consummation—the glorious issue—the full redemption of body and soul forever.

II. Christians have reasons for the hope that is within them. These reasons are many; but we refer to the three chief:

A. *A persuasion of the truth of God's Word.* They hope for these things, because they are revealed in the Scriptures—published and offered there. There the foundation, the medium, and the certainty of salvation, both present and eternal, are made known. Now, the Christian believes most firmly the truth of this volume; he considers it as God's own word, and he rests on it as an immovable rock. "The grass withereth, the flower fadeth, but the word of the Lord endureth forever." Another reason is,

B. *The experience of true religion in the soul.* There is the harmony of their experience with the Word of God. They have tested the Gospel. It is represented as a word of light—and they are enlightened; a word of power—and their rocky hearts have been broken; a word of mercy—and their guilt they feel to be canceled; a word of purity—and their evil hearts are cleansed; a word of comfort and joy—and they have peace; the word of Christ—and Christ is now within their hearts, the hope of glory. Another reason is,

C. *The concurring testimony of all believers.* The experience of one Christian is in the main the testimony of all; the general external and internal effects are the same. Persons of all grades etc., profess to know, to feel, and to enjoy the same. Hence, in the mouths of many witnesses is the reality of religion established.

III. Christians may be called upon to give a reason of their hopes to others.

A. Fellow Christians may ask this for their own edification. "They that feared the Lord . . ."

B. Penitent inquirers may ask, for their direction and encouragement. "They shall come seeking . . . inquiring their way to Zion."

C. Infidels may ask, to scoff and rail at religion. To mock; to gainsay. Now observe,

IV. To these inquirers we are to give an answer.

A. *We must be able to do it*. Not ignorant of the great grounds and principles of our faith and hope. Religion not a blind thing—not mere feeling.

B. *We must be ready to do it*. Have the mind to do it. Not be afraid, nor ashamed, nor reluctant.

C. *We must do it in a right manner*. "With meekness." A calm, quiet spirit; a modest manner. Not ostentatiously; not self-complacently; but with meekness. "With fear"; that is, solemnly—seriously; with reverence for God and the truth. Not flippantly; not with levity.

Application:

1. *Let the Christian rejoice in his hope*. How rich, blessed, and certain! It ought to lift him up; make him always rejoice (Rom. 15:13).

2. *This hope is within the reach of all*. Christ is the hope; He is offered to you.

3. *Do not reject Christianity until you have a substitute*.

Jabez Burns

When hope is in the objective, that is, something set before us, it always refers to Christ's coming for His saints.

1. **"The Hope"** (Col. 1:5). Christ Himself.

2. **"Our Hope"** (1 Tim. 1:1). Common heritage of believers.

3. **"This Hope"** (1 John 3:3). We shall be "like Him."

4. **"Hope of the Gospel"** (Col. 1:23). Revealed by, and part of, the Gospel.

5. **"Hope of Salvation"** (1 Thess. 5:8). Completion of salvation.

6. **"Hope of Righteousness"** (Gal. 5:5). Vindication of the Lord's own.

7. **"Hope of Eternal Life"** (Titus 1:2; 3:7). The blessedness of life eternal in the future.

8. **"Hope of Our Calling"** (Eph. 4:4). What we shall have when Christ comes.

9. **"Hope of His Calling"** (Eph. 1:18). What Christ will have.

10. **"Hope of Glory"** (Col. 1:27). The excellence of His glorious manifestation.

11. **"Living Hope"** (1 Peter 1:3 RV). The lastingness of His livingness.

12. **"Blessed Hope"** (Titus 2:13). Present joy and lasting bliss.

F. E. Marsh

HOPELESSNESS

Having no hope (Eph. 2:12).

What is "hopelessness"?

Godlessness, and being without Christ, must result in "having no hope." Without God there can be no hope. Without Christ there is for the sinner no hope.

To what,

I. Does the text refer?—"Having no hope."

No well-grounded expectation of the Divine favor, or of life in the world to come. All the future a dark impenetrable mist—no foreshadowing of future glory.

II. What are the signs of this condition?

A. Darkness of mind.

B. Unbelief.

C. The servitude of sin.

D. Ungodliness of heart and spirit.

III. The inevitable results of this state.

A. Wretchedness of life.

B. Inward want and dissatisfaction.

C. Gloomy apprehensions of the future.

1. Then let the Gospel be faithfully presented to them.

2. Let them be urged to look to God in Christ, and thus receive the light of joy and hope into the soul.

3. A hopeless condition is a most foreshadowing of the despair and horrors of the second death.

Jabez Burns

DEPRESSION

The problem of depression is the opposite of "hopefulness." It is said that Mr. Spurgeon on one occasion was greatly depressed. One of his officers asked "those who had been converted or blessed under his ministry to rise," and 1,200 rose to their feet. "Now," said the deacon, "I charge you all to pray for your pastor."

Many of God's servants have gotten into the mire of depression, and we have the record of some of their experiences, that we may avoid their depressions.

1. **David**: "I shall one day perish by the hand of Saul" (1 Sam. 27:1).

2. **Job**: "Why died I not from the womb?" (Job 3:11).

3. **Elijah**: "O Lord, take away my life" (1 Kings 19:4).

4. **Moses**: "I am not able to bear all this people" (Num. 11:14).

5. **Psalmist**: "I watch, and am as a sparrow alone upon the housetop" (Ps. 102:7).

6. **Jeremiah**: "Behold, O Lord, for I am in distress" (Lam. 1:20).

7. **Jonah**: "It is better for me to die than to live" (Jonah 4:8).

Discontent and disappointment often lead to discouragement, and discouragement leads to depression, and these together will breed despair. But complete dependence upon God leads to hopefulness and triumph.

F. E. Marsh

BANDS OF LOVE

Hosea 11:4

1. **Christ's Life Illustrates His Love.** See how often He is said to be "moved with compassion" (Matt. 9:36; 14:14; 15:32; 20:34; Mark 1:41; 5:19; Luke 7:13). His life, like the sun in its shining, was beneficent in its ministry.

2. **Christ's Cross Displays His Love.** "He gave Himself up" (Gal. 2:20 RV; Eph. 5:2, 25 RV). Think of what He *gave up*, to what and for whom He gave Himself, and the *outcome* of His giving.

3. **Christ's Grace Confirms His Love.** Believers are loved, loosed, and lifted (Rev. 1:5 RV), and nothing can separate from His love. See the seven things that ordinarily can separate in Romans 8:35; and the ten things that would divide in Romans 8:38–39.

4. **Christ's Truth Affirms His Love.** The words of truth assure us of the continuity of His love (John 13:1), as well as the measure and manner of it (John 15:9, 12).

5. **Christ's Friends Testify to His Love.** His love is particular in its affection (John 11:5), sympathetic in its service (John 11:35), and confiding in its fellowship (John 13:23).

6. **Christ's Spirit Imparts His Love** (Rom. 5:5; 1 John 4:16). He leads to the love that saves, imparts the love that sanctifies, and is the secret of the sacrificing love that serves.

7. **Christ's Operation through us Demonstrates His Love** (2 Cor. 5:14). The constraining power of His love is the moving force to impel in holy service and lowly sacrifice.

F. E. Marsh

LOVE OF THE WHOLE MAN

Thou shalt love the Lord thy God with all thy heart, and with all thy soul, and with all thy strength, and with all thy mind (Luke 10:27).

Duty toward God is summed up in this passage. At first sight it appears to be simple. But it requires the love of our whole being.

1. **Emotional**. "With all thy heart." According to the Jews the heart is the seat of the emotions. The text emphasizes the fact the love of God must be emotional. It need not necessarily be exuberant; it may be calm and steadfast. Many people are worried because they do not experience any sudden uprush of feeling. They need not be. Their love may be calm and gentle. The main point is that it must exist and be felt.

2. **Spiritual**. "With all thy soul." This is love springing from the higher self and involves communion and union with God. It is the state of being spiritually at one with Him.

3. **Physical**. "With all my strength." Strength, with the Jews, was connected with the physical body. The body must be devoted to God as the temple of the Holy Spirit. Love of Him must find expression through the body in acts of love and worship and service.

4. **Intellectual**. "With all thy mind." A wise husband studies his wife and a wise wife her husband. So, too, God must be studied. Time must be devoted to a mental consideration of His attributes, His modes of working, His means of grace, and to His Holy Word. There must be an endeavor made to assimilate, mentally, to the utmost capacity of the mind His revelation of Himself.

We must love God, then, with our whole being. That love must be a true expression of our attitude toward him.

Selected

HOW TO CREATE CHRISTIAN LOVE

This is my commandment, That ye love one another, as I have loved you (John 15:12).

People say there are ten commandments, forgetting this one, the eleventh. In it Christ shows how to create Christian love. It is by loving as He loved.

I. Here is a statement made. It is that God loves us. We cannot doubt this fact. But it will do us good to consider in what ways Christ loved His apostles and all the world.
   A. He loved with an inspiring love.
   B. He loved with an affection that wept over their errors.
   C. He loved with a love that forgave.
   D. He loved with a love that lifted.
   E. He loved with a sympathetic love.
   F. He loved with a love that was willing to die for men. The standard of human love is set for us in the divine love.

II. Here is a command given. It is that we love each other as He has loved us. Following Christ's example, we must love our fellow men with an inspiring love, with a love that weeps over their faults, with a love that forgives their sins against us, with a love that lifts them out of the mire, that sympathizes with them in their misfortunes, and that would even dare to die that they may live.

III. This kind of love, Christian love, becomes the mastering force of the world. Men refuse to follow us when we show our strength. But when we go out into the world with a warm heart they will follow. It is not by might, not by power, but by Christian love we shall conquer, leading men from darkness into light. This kind of love will settle all national, racial and individual problems. Learn to love as Jesus loved.

D. W. Haskew

LOVE SHOWN IN THE MUTUAL
CARE OF CHRISTIANS

Whether one member suffer, all the members suffer with it; or one member be honored, all members rejoice with it (1 Cor. 12:26).

The circumstances and varied gifts of the church at Corinth.

1. Note the diversity of the church. All nations and races of men. All kinds and conditions of men. All gifts and graces fitting for every form of service in Christ's name. Yet all this diversity is in unity, ministered by one and the same Spirit. Paul illustrates this in the human body.

2. Note also the unity of the church. When we see Christians being martyred in the East we all suffer, are aroused. The size of the body in no way deadens the pain of its members. The same locally. We have one church, many members. We have concern for the least, as well as the most prominent. Little faults in members pain the whole body. Illustration, a speck in the eye or a splinter in the hand.

3. The church's care of its members. How deal with the problems? Condemn the finger because of the splinter? Cut it off? No. It is your member. It suffers, you suffer. You exhaust means rather than lose the member. "Now ye are the body of Christ, and members in particular." For progress in sister churches in our city we are glad. Since all are members of Christ's body, He too rejoices. There is joy in heaven. Evidently there is nothing that can be more unifying, more blessed, than genuine Christian faith and fellowship. This whole matter of relationships in the church can be summed up in the word "love." Love underlies all other godly attitudes.

Selected

LIVING IN LOVE

Overcome evil with good (Rom. 12:21).

1. We are not to render evil for evil, but to love our neighbor and even our enemy. Love and hate are two antagonistic principles. Mercy crowns legalism with salvation as light dispels darkness and love extinguishes hate.

2. The spirit of Christ is that of gentleness, meekness, and overwhelming love. The leaves of some trees cannot be whipped off in the winter, but when the sap begins to rise in the spring, they fall to the ground. Developing the good eliminates the evil; exalting Jesus is better than fighting Satan; he falls as Christ rises.

3. Cultivating the good prevents the growth of sin. The tonic of sunlight and pure air is often better than medicine; so keeping in the love of God vitalizes the character to resist sin. Excrescences of the soul drop off while growing in the Christian life. Therefore, attack evil from heaven rather than from the earth. "If thine enemy hunger, feed him." The expulsive power of a new affection will help the enemy to love the friend.

   It is said that a bullet will not go far in a sandbank; it is checked with the gentle resistance of a kiss, but it would penetrate much farther through hard wood.

4. Yielding is more overcoming than hateful resistance. Love is God's way.

Selected

KEEP OUT OF DEBT

Owe no man anything, but to love one another (Rom. 13:8).

Aberdeen, Scotland, for many years had a minister, trusted and beloved, who was a bit different in many ways. He made strange and unexpected departures from the ritual. For example, in the wedding ceremony, he injected questions of his own. He would turn to the groom and inquire, "What makes a good husband?" He had his own answer and would quickly give it and ask the young man to repeat it: "The grace of God and keeping out of debt."

I.   That does make a good husband, a good church, a good home.

II.   However, there is one way in which we are forever in debt: love is a debt that can never be paid. Love is an honorable debt, an obligation we are proud to confess.

III.   "God so loved the world, that he gave." Let us so practice love that we shall have no difficulty about debt.

Bruce S. Wright

A LOVE GIFT

Mary therefore took a pound of ointment of pure nard, very precious, and anointed the feet of Jesus, and wiped his feet with her hair (John 12:3 RV).

Gifts may be made through fear, duty, or love. This on the part of Mary was a true love gift.

I.   The essence of Christianity is love. "We know we have passed from death unto life because we love."

A. A Christian will love his enemies. Should love a sinner, but not his sins. Love an enemy, but not that which makes him your enemy. Malice, envy, hate are lusts of the flesh and foreign to Christ.

B. A Christian will love the brethren. "Little children, love one another."

II.   The end of love is service.

A. Love finds supreme joy in giving. One may give without loving, he cannot love without giving. The more we love, the more self-sacrificing our gift.

B. Mary's gift was one of love. She had found great joy in Jesus' presence at all times. Her brother had lately been restored to her from the grave. Mr. Barclay, missionary to Morocco, saved the life of a young man who had been condemned to death. The mother,

---

a stranger, ran into the road as he was passing, removed his foot from the stirrup, and kissed it passionately. Compare Mary's love. We serve Christ by serving those whom He loves.

Selected

THE NEW COMMANDMENT

A new commandment I give unto you, that you love one another, as I have loved you (John 13:34).

We all know the Ten Commandments. Is there another besides? Yes. This one is new. Why is it called new? For one reason, because it is founded on a new relation, our relation to Christ. And this relation to Christ involves a new relation to each other. We are brethren, members of one family. "As many as received him, to them gave he power to become the sons of God."

I. **It is Christ's commandment.** It belongs to His parting instructions to His church. How are His followers to vanquish all opposition of the world? Not by amassing wealth. Not by seeking high offices. Not by equiping fleets and armies. Not by employing craft and intrigue. No, the power was to be that of love.
    A. Love as a principle of life.
    B. Love as an impulse to sacrifice.

II. **Its novelty. "A new commandment I give."**
    A. It is historically new.
    B. It is new in extent.
    C. It is new in its comprehensiveness.

III. **Its measure and meaning.**
    A. Complete sympathy.
    B. Utter self-sacrifice. "As I have loved you." "Greater love hath no man than this, that a man lay down his life for his friends." Love, how attentive! Love, how confiding! Love, how compassionate! Love, how disinterested! Love, how self-sacrificing!

Selected

THE BADGE OF DISCIPLESHIP

*By this shall all men know that you are my disciples, if you have love
one to another (John 13:35).*

Read the thirteenth chapter of First Corinthians. The badge of
discipleship is love.

**I. The importance of a correct recognition of this. "By
this shall all men know."**
   A. It is important for the credit of the Gospel.
   B. It is important for the influence of a good life.
   C. Brotherly love is important that reproach fall not upon
the church.
   D. That hypocrisy may be exposed.
   E. That Christ may be truly represented.

II. Mutual love is the badge of discipleship.
   A. It is an actual inward experience.
   B. And the principle is manifest in the life.
   C. Its measure is the love of Christ to us.

Selected

LOVE IS OF GOD

Beloved, let us love one another: for love is of God; and every
one that loveth is born of God, and knoweth God (1 John 4:7–8).
Love is the evidence of life in Christ (1 John 3:14).
Love is the first "fruit of the Spirit" (Gal. 5:22).
Love is the activity of faith (Gal. 5:6).
Love is the "fulfilling of the law" (Rom. 8:10).
Love is the "new commandment" (John 13:34).
Love is the debt we owe one another (Rom. 13:8).
Love is the proof of true "discipleship" (John 13:35).
Love is the test of pastoral qualification (Jonn 21:15).
Love is the "bond of perfectness" (Col. 3:14).
Love is more precious than earthly riches (Song of Sol. 8:7).
Love is strong as death (Song of Sol. 8:6).
Love is not to be in *word* only. Love is to be in *deed* and in
truth (1 John 3:18).

Love is to be fervent, out of a pure heart (1 Peter 1:22).
Love is to abound yet more and more (1 Thess. 3:12).
Love constrains to self-denying service (2 Cor. 5:14).
Love becometh "dear children" (Eph. 5:1–2.
Love will cover a multitude of sins (Prov. 10:12).
Love suffereth long and is kind. Love envieth not. Love vaunteth not itself. Love is not puffed up. Love doth not behave itself unseemly. Love seeketh not her own. Love is not easily offended. Love thinketh no evil. Love rejoiceth not in iniquity. Love rejoiceth in the truth. Love beareth all things. Love believeth all things. Love hopeth all things. Love endureth all things. Love never faileth (1 Cor. 13).

"This is love, that we walk after His commandments."

THE LOVE OF THE INFINITE GOD

The love of the Father (John 3:16; 1 John 4:8–10)
The love of the Son (Gal. 2:20; Eph. 5:2; John 15:19).
The love of the Spirit (Rom. 15:30).

Selected

LOVE: OUR RELATIVE DUTY TO BELIEVERS

A new commandment I give unto you, that ye love one another: as I have loved you, that ye also love one another (John 13:34).

Now are they many members, yet but one body (2 Cor. 12:20).

Ye ought to wash one another's feet (John 13:14).

Be kindly affectioned one to another (Rom. 12:10).

In honor preferring one another (Rom. 12:10).

Be of the same mind one toward another (Rom. 12:16).

Receive ye one another, as Christ also received us to the glory of God (Rom. 15:7).

By love serve one another (Gal. 5:13).

Bear ye one another's burdens (Gal. 6:2).

Be ye kind one to another, tenderhearted (Eph. 4:32).

Forgive one another (Eph. 4:32).

Forbearing one another (Col. 3:13).

Teaching and admonishing one another (Col. 3:16).

Comfort one another (1 Thess. 4:18).

Edify one another (1 Thess. 5:11).

And let us consider one another to provoke unto love and to good works (Heb. 10:24).

Exhorting one another, and so much the more as ye see the day approaching (Heb. 10:25).

Confess your faults one to another (James 5:16).

Pray for one another (James 5:16).

Having compassion one of another (1 Peter 3:8).

Use hospitality one to another (1 Peter 4:9).

All of you be subject one to another (1 Peter 5:5).

Beloved let us love one another, for love is of God (1 John 4:7).

Selected

GOD IS LOVE

He calls us sons (1 John 3:1).

His love is everlasting (Jer. 31:3).

He is for us (Rom. 8:31).

He gave His Son for us (John 3:16; Rom. 8:32).

Who shall separate us from the love (Rom. 8:35).

Nothing shall be able . . . (Rom. 8:39).

We are safe in His love (no man) (John 10:28).

The extent of His love (unto the end) (John 13:1; 1 Thess. 5:18; Ps. 69:30; 1 Peter 2:15; Eph. 2:10; John 14:23; Matt. 7:21; Luke 12:47; James 4:17).

The end—Everlasting Life (1 John 2:17; Col. 4:12; Eph. 4:13; Heb. 13:20–21; 2 Cor. 9:8; John 17:24; Rev. 3:4; Rev. 22:3–4; 1 Thess. 4:17).

Selected

LOVE'S ATTITUDE

Waiting for the coming (revelation) of our Lord Jesus Christ (1 Cor. 1:7).

Fiction has painted the picture of a maiden whose lover left her for a voyage to the Holy Land, promising on his return to make her his beloved bride. Many told her that she would never see him again.

But she believed his word and evening by evening she went down to the lonely shore, and kindled there a beacon light in sight of the roaring waves to hail and welcome the returning ship which was to bring again her betrothed. And by that watch fire she took her stand each night, praying to the winds to hasten on the sluggish sails, that he who was everything to her might come. Even so that blessed Lord, who has loved us to death, has gone away to the mysterious holy land of heaven, promising on His return to make us His happy and eternal Bride. Some say that He has gone forever, and that here we shall never see Him more. But His last word was, "Yea, I come quickly," and on the dark and misty beach sloping out into the eternal sea, each true believer stands by the love-lit fire, looking and waiting and praying, and hoping for the fulfillment of His Word, in nothing gladder than in His pledge and promise, and calling ever from the soul of sacred love, "Even so, come, Lord Jesus."

Some of these nights, while the world is busy with its merry frivolities, and laughing at the maiden on the shore, a form shall rise over the surging waves, as once on Galilee, to vindicate forever all this watching and devotion, and bring to the faithful and constant heart a joy and glory and triumph which never more shall end.

The attitude of the believer to the Lord's return evidences our faithfulness to Him.

I. **We should look for Him expectantly (Titus 2:13).**

II. **Watch for Him faithfully (Luke 12:35–48).**

III. **Wait for Him ardently (Phil. 3:20–21).**

IV. **Love Him supremely (2 Tim. 4:8).**

V. **Occupy for Him diligently (Luke 19:13).**

VI. **Remember Him thankfully (1 Cor. 11:26).**

VII. **Yield to Him wholly (1 Thess. 5:23).**

F. E. Marsh

LOVE'S MINISTRY

The Love of Christ constraineth us (2 Cor. 5:14).

A well-known editor says, "The greatest, if not the most beautiful thing I ever saw, was in the city of Edinburgh. A boy saw that his little sister's stockingless feet were cold, so he took off his cap and said to her, 'Maggie, your feet are cold, put them in my cap.'" A capless head meant covered feet, and doubtless, a "cold" head was the result of warmed feet.

Surely the incident tells us what love loves to do. A heart of love ever expresses itself in a hand of labor.

I. Love "covers a multitude of sins" (1 Peter 4:8 RV).

II. Feeds the sheep and lambs (John 21:15–17).

III. Forbears with another's weakness (Eph. 5:2).

IV. Sacrifices what is its own (1 Sam. 17:1–31).

V. Ministers to another's need (1 John 3:17).

VI. Gives up its rights (Ex. 21:5).

VII. Overcomes difficulties (Song of Sol. 8:7).

VIII. Is longsuffering in its kindness (1 Cor. 13:4).

F. E. Marsh

LOVE'S MINISTRY

He loved . . . He gave (John 3:16).

A well-known writer has described the ministry of true love as follows, "To give! To give without hope of recompense, without question, without fear! That was the message of life." Who is there that answers to the ideal in all its reality? Certainly there was One who did, and that One was Christ. He gave "without hope of recompense." His recompense was in giving.

Love gives out of its own nature, and cannot do any other than it does. It is not occupied with its own beneficence, for it is absorbed in its service. Christ gave "without question," and "without fear." He did not reason why? His was to do and die. The threats of men did not daunt Him, nor did the hate of hell deter Him. In the absorbing passion of His Father's will, and in the pursuit of reaching the Father's goal of glory, He kept steadily on. What a "message of life" He gives us, and what an Example for imitation He leaves us. Can we imitate Him?

We make the attempt, and soon we find ourselves like Peter "following afar"! If the ideal of His perfect love is to be an actuality in us in any way, He must make it actual; only He can. The Christ within in His life must walk in the life He lived outwardly.

Christ ever went about doing good, and virtue was going out of Him all the time. Luke 24 is one of the many chapters where Christ's activities are recorded.

1. **Love's Approach**—"Jesus Himself drew near" (v. 15). Christ is ever coming to us that He may make Himself known, and He always comes with some definite blessing.

2. **Love's Announcements**—"He said" (vv. 17, 19, 25, 36, 38, 44, 46). His messages are ever meaningful and soul-making. He sometimes rebukes in His love that He may bless in His grace.

3. **Love's Association**—"He expounded . . . the Scriptures . . . concerning Himself" (v. 27). The Living and the Written Word go together. We need Him to reveal to us the association.

4. **Love's Aside**—"He made as though He would go further" (v. 28). His seeming withdrawals are made to draw us out and on, and that we may pray "Abide with us."

5. **Love's Abiding**—"He went in to tarry" ("Abide," v. 29 RV). Prayer answered means His abiding, and that means all we need.

6. **Love's Attention**—"He sat . . . took . . . blessed . . . brake, and gave" (v. 30). He feeds, and blesses, and gives; and He does all that we may know Him (v. 31). He loves to make Himself known, and knowing Him, our hearts are at rest.

7. **Love's Assimilation**—"He vanished. . . ." "He talked . . ." "He opened" (vv. 31–32). He left the aroma of His presence behind, and He fused the hearts of the disciples into

one, for they felt He had assimilated their hearts into one—"our heart."

8. **Love's Appearance**—"The Lord . . . appeared to Simon" (v. 34). The Lord knew the anguish of heart Peter was in, so He made a special visit to him and restored him from his backsliding state.

9. **Love's Attractability**—"Jesus Himself stood in the midst. . . ." "He saith, Peace. . . ." "It is I Myself. . . ." "He showed them His hands and His feet. . . ." "Joy" (vv. 36–41). He was the Center around whom the disciples gathered, and He Himself was the Joy of their hearts.

10. **Love's Affirmation**—"I spake." "Opened He" (vv. 44–45). He not only reminded them of what He said, but He confirmed it by opening the Scriptures and by opening their understanding. His affirmations are always confirmations and benedictions.

11. **Love's Authority**—"I send" (v. 49). He sends the Holy Spirit as He promised that we may know His authority and ability to carry out His pledges.

12. **Love's Action**—"He led" (v. 50). His leadings are for our good and His givings.

13. **Love's Attitude**—"He blessed them" (vv. 50–51). Those nailed-printed hands are uplifted for our blessing. Gaze on those hands and hear them speak.

14. **Love's Adorableness**—"They worshiped Him" (v. 52). We must adore Him in worship when we behold His adorableness.

F. E. Marsh

LOVE'S TRAITS

God is Love (1 John 4:8).

Dr. John G. Paton had a bad character to deal with in his New Hebrides mission in a Tanna man named Nasi. Mr. H. O. Cady tells of a serious illness which befell Nasi and during which Dr. Paton ministered to him regularly, but no kindness seemed to move him. After the doctor had sailed for home, a band of native Christians held a consultation over the case of Nasi. They said, "We know the burden and trouble that Nasi has been to our dear pastor; we know that he has murdered several persons with his own hands, and has taken part in the murder of others. Let us unite in daily prayer that the Lord will open his heart and change his conduct, and teach him to love and follow what is good, and let us set ourselves to win him for Christ just as we were won." So they began to show him every possible kindness, one after another helping daily. At first he repelled them and sullenly held aloof, but prayer never ceased and love grew. At last Nasi broke down, and said, "I can oppose Jesus no longer. If He can make you treat me like that, I yield myself to Him and to you. I want Him to change me; I want a heart like that of Jesus," and when Dr. Paton returned from his furlough he found this former murderer a devoted, loving follower of Jesus.

The Essence of God's Nature "is Love." Love with Him is not an attribute, it is what He "*is*"; but as there are seven colors to the rainbow, so there are seven traits of Love.

1. **"Compassion" is the *Heart* of Love.** When the father saw the prodigal, his heart was "moved with compassion" (Luke 15:20). His inner being was stirred to its depths, and showed itself in the kiss of forgiveness, the clasp of affection, the robe of adornment, the shoes of protection, the ring of honor, the feast of provision, the words of appreciation, and the joy of gladness.

2. **"Kindness" is the *Act* of Love.** "The kindness," as well as "the love of God," appeared (Titus 3:4). When David would express his regard, to Mephibosheth, he did it for Jonathan's sake (2 Sam. 9:3–7), and showed his beneficence in what he did for him. So God, for Christ's sake, blesses us.

3. **"Grace" is the *Generosity* of Love.** Grace does not look at the deserts of the object upon which it shows its favor, but gives everything for nothing, when the recipient does not deserve anything. The grace came through Christ (John 1:17), and enriches those who were poor (2 Cor. 8:9).

4. **"Mercy" is the *Disposition* of Love.** "God, who is rich in mercy, for His great love wherewith He hath loved us" (Eph. 2:4). We sometimes sing that "Love moved the mighty God"; but that is not so—He moved because He loved. His hands of mercy are extended toward us, because His heart of love determined to save us (Titus 3:5).

5. **"Sacrifice" is the *Service* of Love.** When the saints are exhorted to "walk in love," they are pointed to Him who "loved us, and hath given Himself for us, an offering and a sacrifice to God for a sweet-smelling savor" (Eph. 5:2). Love will sacrifice much for the object of its affection, as Jonathan did for David (1 Sam. 18:1–4), but it thinks not of the sacrifice it makes.

6. **"Pity" is the *Help* of Love.** When Jehovah acted for His people, we read, "In His love and pity He redeemed them, and He bare them, and carried them all the days of old" (Isa. 63:9). Humans pity one another, but do not always help. God's pity shows itself in help and sympathy. Pity frees from bondage, carries our load, and is not weary in helping.

7. **"Sympathy" is the *Fellowship* of Love.** "Bowels of mercies" is expressive of the feeling of tender regard which one has for another (Gen. 43:30; Phil. 1:8; Col. 3:12; Philem. 7, 12, 20; 1 John 3:17). The tears of Christ revealed His heart of sympathetic love. To weep with another is to express the feeling one has for the other.

F. E. Marsh

LOVE'S RECOGNITION

I know Him, whom I have believed (2 Tim. 1:12 RV).

Children are ever helpful in the expression of their faith and the devotion of their love. The following incident is a practical illustration. A little girl, whose Sunday school teacher had died some time before, had a dream that she was in heaven, and went around being introduced by her friend to several well-known characters. The girl, in relating the dream of her mother, said, "My teacher introduced me to Paul, and Abraham, and David, and a lot of other Bible characters."

"Did she not introduce you to Jesus?" asked the mother.

"Oh, no," was the prompt reply, "I knew Jesus as soon as I saw Him, I did not need an introduction to Him."

Those who have been introduced to Christ by the Holy Spirit, do not need any further introduction to Him, for the moment we see Him we shall know Him.

> By the *nail-prints* of His atonement (Zech. 13:6).
> By the *glory-face* of His splendor (Rev. 22:4).
> By the *lifting-power* of His attractability (1 Thess. 4:17).
> By the *welcome-voice* of His greeting (Song of Sol. 2:10).
> By the *corresponding-likeness* to His face (Phil. 3:21).
> By the *love-companionship* of His presence (1 Thess. 4:17).
> By the *unsurpassed-following* of His retinue (Rev. 19:11–14).

To know Christ is the secret of power; to win Christ is the secret of growth; to love Christ is the secret of joy; to abide in Christ is the secret of victory; to follow Christ is the secret of faith; to listen to Christ is the secret of knowledge; and to walk with Christ is the secret of rest.

F. E. Marsh

LOVE'S MANTLE

Love covereth a multitude of sins (1 Peter 4:8 RV).

The artist of Alexander the Great was very desirous of producing a faithful portrait of the great general, but he was anxious to hide the ugly scar upon the side of his face which was the telltale of a wound received in one of his battles. He, therefore, represented the great conqueror in a reflective mood, with his head resting upon his hand, and his forefinger covering the disfiguring scar. Love ever seeks to cover the scars which are the marks left by the old master sin.

How does love cover sin? Certainly not aiding others in sin, nor by minimizing its evil, nor by excusing its iniquity. How, then?

I. By acting toward others, as God has acted toward us, in a forgiving spirit (Ps. 32:5), as Joseph did to his brethren (Gen. 45:4–15).

II. By seeking to heal the effects of sin in the repentant sinner, by pouring into his heart and mind the oil of prayerful sympathy and the joy of encouragement, as the good Samaritan did to the spoiled man (Luke 10:34).

III. By seeking to remove the shame which another's folly has brought upon him, as Noah's sons did when they discovered their father in a drunken condition and covered him up (Gen. 9:23).

IV. By restoring a brother who has fallen, in the spirit of Christ, that he may be prevented from being tripped up again, as Paul sought to restore and to guide the church at Corinth in their conduct toward the erring brother (1 Cor. 5:5; 2 Cor. 2:7–8).

V. By rescuing those who are liable to sin through unholy associations, as the angels did Lot (Gen. 19:10–11).

VI. By removing temptation out of the way of those who are weak, by our personal example, as the Holy Spirit directs in Romans 14.

VII. By refusing to talk about the past of anyone who has repented, whether it be saint or sinner, as the Lord Himself, who not only forgives, but forgets too (Heb. 10:17).

The love of God is a torrent to bear us on in its sweep; love is a channel to hem us in, in its sway; and an ocean to embrace us in its fullness. Love is a power to move us, a sphere to limit us, and a fullness to enrich us.

F. E. Marsh